378

First paperback edition 1998

First published 1995 in hardback by
A&C Black (Publishers) Limited,
35 Bedford Row, London WC1R 4JH

ISBN 0-7136-5020-6
A CIP catalogue record for this book is available
from the British Library.

Acknowledgements

Photographs by Zul Mukhida, except page 17;
Eye Ubiquitous.

Design by Helen White.

Photographic and design direction by
Karen Bryant-Mole.

The author and publisher would like to thank all
the children who appear in the photographs.

Printed and bound by Partenaires Fabrication,
Malesherbes, France.

Is it shiny?

Karen Bryant-Mole

A&C Black • London

liquid

Yasmin is pouring out some milk.
Things that can be poured are **liquids**.

solid

Now she is eating some cake.
Cake can't be poured. It is a **solid**.

hard

Tim knocks on the door.
The door feels **hard**.

soft

He goes inside and takes off his shoes.
The fluffy rug feels **soft**.

stretchy

Lou has some **stretchy** braces.
When he pulls them, they get longer.

springy

This **springy** foam ball
can go back to its proper shape.

wet

Sarah has been swimming.
Her costume is all **wet**.

dry

Sarah has changed into some **dry** clothes.

rough

This pineapple feels **rough**.
Its skin is bumpy.

smooth

A mango has a **smooth** skin.
The skin feels flat.

rigid

This spaghetti hasn't been cooked yet.
It is stiff and **rigid**.

bendy

Cooked spaghetti is **bendy**.
Thomas can wind it round his fork.

shiny

Yasmin is wearing a bright, **shiny** raincoat.

dull

Lou's raincoat is not shiny.
It is **dull**.

furry

Sarah likes to stroke her cat.
Its coat feels soft and **furry**.

prickly

This hedgehog has **prickly** spikes.
If you touch them, they feel sharp.

patterned

Lou's shorts are **patterned**.
There are lots of different shapes on them.

plain

Vusa's jumper is all one colour.
There are no shapes on it. It is **plain**.

gritty

Sand is made from tiny pieces of rock.
It feels rough and **gritty**.

powdery

Powdery things, like talcum powder,
feel soft and smooth.

transparent

You can see through Vusa's glass.
Her glass is **transparent**.

opaque

You can't see through Yasmin's tumbler.
It is **opaque**.

Index

This index will help you find the Buzzwords in this book.

Things to do

Collections
You could make collections of different types of objects, such as shiny objects or smooth objects. Decorate old shoe boxes and use them to store your collections. Glue one of the objects on to each lid, to remind yourself what sort of things are inside.

Ice-cubes
Is it solid or is it liquid? Ask a grown-up to help you make some fruit juice ice-cubes. When you pour the juice into the ice-cube tray it is a liquid. Once it has frozen, it can't be poured, so it must be a solid. What happens if you put the frozen cubes into a cup and leave them for a while?

Model
Try making junk models, thinking about the best materials to use. Egg boxes are good for a crocodile's rough skin. Foil would make a robot look shiny. A soft rabbit's tail could be made from cotton wool.

What am I thinking of ?
Play this guessing game with your friends. Describe an object using only Buzzwords. For example, 'I'm thinking of something hard and transparent.' See if your friends can guess what you are thinking of.

How to use this book

Children's understanding of concepts is fundamentally linked to their ability to comprehend and use relevant language. This book is designed to help children understand the vocabulary associated with materials.

Materials are an important area within science. They are the foundation upon which chemistry is built. Materials can be man-made, like plastic and glass, or natural, like sand and water.

Grouping materials and describing their properties are essential scientific skills. This book helps children develop those skills by explaining key words connected to the properties of materials and by encouraging children to look for similarities and differences between objects.

Each word in the book is explained through a colour photograph, which illustrates it, and a phrase which uses that word in context.

Some of the pairs of words featured on each double page are opposites, such as **hard** and **soft.** Other pairs of words, such as **furry** and **prickly** are not opposites. Children can be encouraged to discuss which pairs are opposites and which are not.

As well as explaining words that are basic to the understanding of materials and their properties, the book can be used in a number of other ways.

Children can think of, or find, objects other than the one in the photograph that can be described using a particular Buzzword. The Buzzword, **opaque**, does not just describe tumblers. It can be applied to a wide variety of types of object. Teddy bears, tree trunks, pencils, apples and jumpers are all opaque.

The book can be used to help a child define the properties of a particular object. Materials can often be described using more than one word. A stone, for instance, might be described as hard, smooth, plain, dull and opaque.

Children can be encouraged to think about the uses of the different properties and how this makes them suitable for particular functions. Why is stretchy elastic best for braces? Why is hard wood good for doors? How do prickly spikes protect hedgehogs?

The properties of materials and objects aren't always constant. Water is a liquid but can be frozen into a solid. Clay is soft but when it is baked it becomes hard. Clothes in a washing machine are wet but when they are hung on the line they become dry. Children can think about whether the properties of particular materials always stay the same. If not, how and why do they change?